FUNKY CHICKEN
Enchiladas

and Other Mexican Dishes

by Nick Fauchald   illustrated by Ronnie Rooney

Special thanks to our content adviser:
Joanne L. Slavin, Ph.D., R.D.
Professor of Food Science and Nutrition
University of Minnesota

PICTURE WINDOW BOOKS
Minneapolis, Minnesota

Editors: Shelly Lyons and Christianne Jones   Designer: Tracy Davies
Page Production: Melissa Kes

Art Director: Nathan Gassman   Editorial Director: Nick Healy
The illustrations in this book were created with watercolor and pen and ink.

Picture Window Books • 151 Good Counsel Drive • P.O. Box 669 • Mankato, MN 56002-0669
877-845-8392 • www.picturewindowbooks.com

The illustration on page 4 is from *www.mypyramid.gov.*

Printed in the United States of America.

Library of Congress Cataloging-in-Publication Data
Fauchald, Nick.
Funky chicken enchiladas and other Mexican dishes / by Nick Fauchald ; illustrated by Ronnie Rooney.
p. cm. — (Kids Dish)
Includes index.
ISBN 978-1-4048-5189-4 (library binding)
1. Cookery, Mexican—Juvenile literature. I. Rooney, Ronnie, ill. II. Title.
TX716.M4F3755 2009
641.5972—dc22   2008037907

Editor's note: The author based the difficulty levels of the recipes on the skills and time required, as well as the number of ingredients and tools needed. Adult help and supervision is required for all recipes.

Table of Contents

EASY

INTERMEDIATE

ADVANCED

MyPyramid

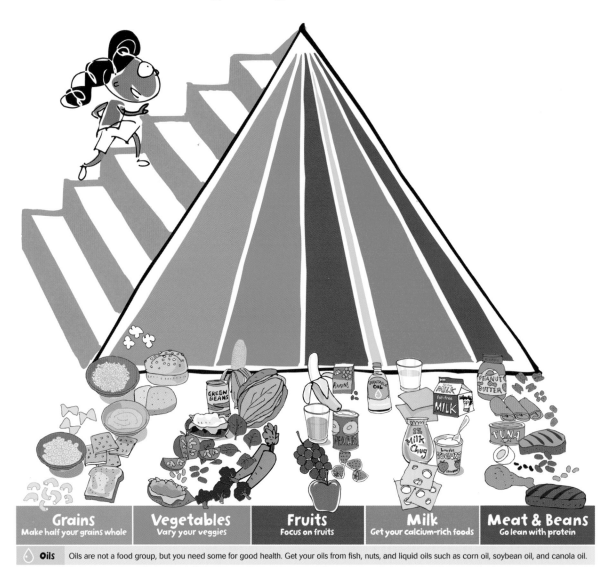

Grains Make half your grains whole	Vegetables Vary your veggies	Fruits Focus on fruits	Milk Get your calcium-rich foods	Meat & Beans Go lean with protein

◊ Oils Oils are not a food group, but you need some for good health. Get your oils from fish, nuts, and liquid oils such as corn oil, soybean oil, and canola oil.

In 2005, the U.S. government created MyPyramid, a plan for healthy eating and living. The new MyPyramid plan contains 12 separate diet plans based on your age, gender, and activity level. For more information about MyPyramid, visit *www.mypyramid.gov.*

The pyramid at the top of each recipe shows the main food groups included. Use the index to find recipes that include food from the food group of your choice, major ingredients used, recipe levels, and appliances/equipment needed.

New York-based **Nick Fauchald** is the author of numerous children's books. He helped create the magazine *Every Day with Rachael Ray* and has been an editor at *Food & Wine* and *Wine Spectator* magazines. Nick attended the French Culinary Institute in Manhattan and has worked with some of the world's best chefs. However, he still thinks kids are the most fun to cook with.

Dear kids,

You probably eat tacos, burritos, and tortilla chips all the time. But there are many other great dishes that come from Mexico, a country with a rich food culture dating back thousands of years. This cookbook will show you how to make many traditional Mexican dishes at home, with only a little help from an adult. Enjoy your meal, or as they say in Mexico, "Buen provecho!"

Cooking is fun, and safety in the kitchen is very important. As you begin your cooking adventure, please remember these tips:

★ Make sure an adult is in the kitchen with you.
★ Tie back your hair and tuck in all loose clothing.
★ Read the recipe from start to finish before you begin.
★ Wash your hands before you start and whenever they get messy.
★ Wash all fresh fruits and vegetables.
★ Take your time cutting the ingredients.
★ Use oven mitts whenever you are working with hot foods or equipment.
★ Stay in the kitchen the entire time you are cooking.
★ Clean up when you are finished.

Now, choose a recipe that sounds tasty, check with an adult, and get cooking. Your friends and family are hungry!

Enjoy,
Nick

KIDS DISH

Note to Adults:

Learning to cook is an exciting, challenging adventure for young people. It helps kids build confidence; learn responsibility; become familiar with food and nutrition; practice math, science, and motor skills; and follow directions. Here are some ways you can help kids get the most out of their cooking experiences:

• Encourage them to read the entire recipe before they begin cooking. Make sure they have everything they need and understand all of the steps.

• Make sure young cooks have a kid-friendly workspace. If your kitchen counter is too high for them, offer them a step stool or a table to work at.

• Expect new cooks to make a little mess, and encourage them to clean it up when they are finished.

• Help multiple cooks divide the tasks before they begin.

• Enjoy what the kids just cooked together.

Special Tips and Glossary

beating egg whites: Using a whisk or fork, stir the egg whites quickly until they have a froth.

cracking eggs: Tap the egg on the counter until it cracks. Hold the egg over a small bowl. Gently pull the two halves of the shell apart until the egg falls into the bowl.

measuring dry ingredients: Measure dry ingredients (such as flour and sugar) by spooning the ingredient into a measuring cup until it's full. Then level off the top of the cup with the back of a butter knife.

measuring wet ingredients: Place a clear measuring cup on a flat surface, then pour the liquid into the cup until it reaches the correct measuring line. Be sure to check the liquid at eye level.

shucking corn: Holding an ear of corn in one hand, peel each of the green leaves from the corn. Once all of the leaves are removed, pull all of the silky threads off of the corn as well.

blend: mix together completely

cool: set hot food on a wire rack until it's no longer hot

line: cover the inside of

mash: smash, usually with a fork, until the food is soft and separated

preheat: turn an oven on before you use it; it usually takes about 15 minutes to preheat an oven

roll: flatten with a rolling pin

sprinkle: scatter something in small bits

stir: mix ingredients with a spoon until blended

toss: mix ingredients together with your hands or two spoons until blended

whisk: stir a mixture rapidly until it's smooth

METRIC CONVERSION CHART

1/4 teaspoon (1 milliliter)
1/2 teaspoon (2.5 milliliters)
1 teaspoon (5 milliliters)
1 1/2 teaspoons (7.5 milliliters)
2 teaspoons (10 milliliters)

1 tablespoon (15 milliliters)
2 tablespoons (30 milliliters)
3 tablespoons (45 milliliters)

1/4 cup (60 milliliters)
1/3 cup (80 milliliters)

1/2 cup (120 milliliters)
3/4 cup (180 milliliters)
1 cup (240 milliliters)
1 1/4 cups (300 milliliters)
1 1/2 cups (360 milliliters)
2 cups (480 milliliters)
3 cups (720 milliliters)

4 ounces (112 grams)
8 ounces (224 grams)
12 ounces (336 grams)
14 ounces (392 grams)

16 ounces (448 grams)
18 ounces (504 grams)

TEMPERATURE CONVERSION CHART

350° Fahrenheit (177° Celsius)
375° Fahrenheit (191° Celsius)
400° Fahrenheit (204° Celsius)
425° Fahrenheit (218° Celsius)

Kitchen Tools

HERE ARE THE TOOLS YOU'LL USE WHEN COOKING THE RECIPES IN THIS BOOK★

8-by-11-inch glass baking dish

9-by-13-inch baking pan

rimmed baking sheets

blender

butter knife

cooking spray

cooling rack

cutting board

drinking glasses

kitchen shears

fork

serving bowls

measuring cups

measuring spoons

melon baller

mesh strainer

clear measuring cup

microwave-safe bowls

mixing bowls

oven mitts

parchment paper

metal spatula

pitcher

pastry brush

pizza cutter

platter

plastic wrap

rubber spatula

serrated knife

serving plates

small, sharp knife

spoon

whisk

wooden skewers

wooden spoons

Tortillas are traditionally made with ground corn called maize.

Fiesta Tortilla Chips

INGREDIENTS

ten 6-inch corn tortillas
2 tablespoons vegetable oil
1 1/2 teaspoons salt
1 teaspoon chili powder
salsa or guacamole,
    for serving

TOOLS

kitchen shears
2 rimmed baking sheets
pastry brush
measuring spoons
oven mitts
platter

Preheat the oven to 375°.

With a kitchen shears, cut each tortilla into triangles.

Spread the triangles in a single layer on two rimmed baking sheets.

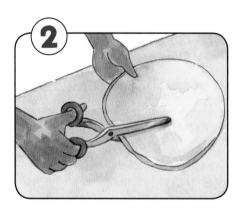

With a pastry brush, lightly brush both sides of each triangle with oil.

NUTRITION NOTE★ Tortilla chips are usually fried in oil. These chips are baked, which makes them a healthier choice than store-bought chips.

5

Sprinkle the triangles with salt and chili powder.

6

Ask an adult to bake the tortilla triangles for 12 to 15 minutes, until they're golden brown and crispy. Rotate the baking sheets halfway through baking.

7 Serve the chips with salsa or guacamole.

FRUITS

In Mexico, *agua fresca*, or "fresh water," is made with all kinds of fruits and vegetables.

Watermelon Agua Fresca

INGREDIENTS
3 cups seedless
   watermelon cubes
1 1/2 cups water
3 tablespoons sugar
3 tablespoons fresh
   lime juice
ice, for serving

TOOLS
clear measuring cup
measuring cups
blender
mesh strainer
pitcher
measuring spoons
wooden spoon
drinking glasses

1 Place the watermelon and water in a blender. Blend until smooth, about 20 seconds.

2 Hold a mesh strainer above a pitcher. Pour the watermelon mixture through the strainer.

3 Add the sugar and lime juice. Stir until the sugar is dissolved.

4 Fill the glasses with ice and agua fresca, and serve.

Salsa verde is Spanish for "green sauce."

Salsa Verde

Remove the husks from the tomatillos. Wash the tomatillos under warm water.

Have an adult cut the tomatillos into quarters.

Place the tomatillos in a blender along with the cilantro and lime juice. Blend until smooth, about 20 seconds.

Pour the tomatillo mixture into a small bowl. Stir in the onion and salt.

5 Serve the salsa verde with tortilla chips.

INGREDIENTS
8 tomatillos,
    husks discarded
1/2 cup cilantro leaves
2 tablespoons fresh lime juice
1/4 cup chopped onion
1/2 teaspoon salt
tortilla chips, for serving

TOOLS
cutting board
serrated knife
blender
measuring cups
measuring spoons
small serving bowl
spoon

FOOD FACT★ Tomatillos are an important ingredient in Mexican cooking. They're in the same family as tomatoes, but they have a tart flavor.

11

This Recipe Includes

GRAINS, MILK, VEGETABLES

Quesadilla means "little cheesy thing" in Spanish.

Cheesy Quesadillas

INGREDIENTS
four 9-inch flour tortillas
one 8-ounce bag shredded
    cheddar cheese
sour cream and salsa,
    for serving

TOOLS
rimmed baking sheet
cooking spray
measuring cups
oven mitts
metal spatula
cutting board
pizza cutter
platter

Preheat the oven to 425°.

Spray a rimmed baking sheet
with cooking spray.

Place two of the tortillas on the
baking sheet.

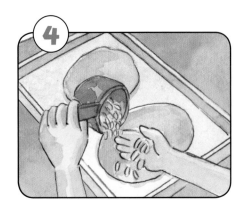

Sprinkle 1 cup of the cheese
evenly over each tortilla.

FUN WITH FOOD★ Turn these quesadillas into a meal
by adding shredded chicken or cooked ground beef.

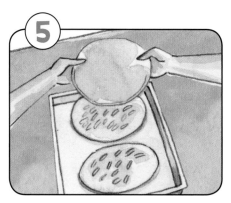

Cover the tortillas with the remaining two tortillas.

Ask an adult to bake the quesadillas for 8 minutes, until lightly brown on top.

With a spatula, flip the quesadillas over and press down lightly. Bake them for 4 more minutes, until the tops are lightly golden and the cheese is melted.

Ask an adult to transfer the quesadillas to a cutting board and cut them into wedges using a pizza cutter.

9 Serve the quesadillas with the sour cream and salsa.

13

Pico de gallo is similar to salsa, but the ingredients are all raw.

Pico de Gallo

INGREDIENTS

1 green pepper
1 bunch fresh cilantro
1 teaspoon chopped garlic
1/2 cup finely chopped
  red onion
2 cups canned chopped
  tomatoes, drained
1 tablespoon fresh
  lime juice
1 teaspoon salt
1/2 teaspoon cumin
tortilla chips, for serving

TOOLS

cutting board
small, sharp knife
kitchen shears
measuring cups
medium-sized mixing bowl
measuring spoons
wooden spoon

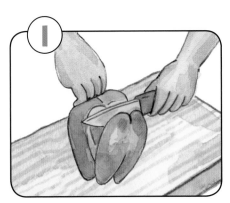

Ask an adult to cut the green pepper in half and remove the seeds.

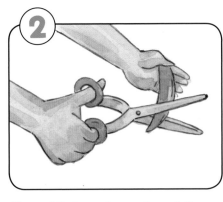

Use a kitchen shears to cut the green pepper into thin strips. Then cut the strips into small pieces.

With a kitchen shears, cut the cilantro into small pieces until you have about 1 cup.

Place the green peppers and cilantro in a medium-sized mixing bowl. Stir in the garlic, onion, and tomatoes.

FOOD FACT★ Pico de gallo makes a great sauce for tacos, as well as cooked fish or chicken.

5 Add the lime juice, salt, and cumin, and stir well.

6 Serve the pico de gallo immediately with chips, or refrigerate it overnight.

This Recipe Includes

VEGETABLES, FRUITS, MILK

This spicy, cheesy corn on the cob is called *elote* in Mexico, where it's a popular street food.

Chili-Cheese Corn on the Cob

INGREDIENTS

4 ears of corn, shucked
1 teaspoon chili powder
1 teaspoon salt
1/4 cup mayonnaise
1 tablespoon fresh
   lime juice
1/2 cup freshly grated
   Parmesan cheese

TOOLS

9-by-13-inch baking pan
oven mitts
2 small mixing bowls
wooden spoon
measuring spoons
whisk
measuring cups
pastry brush
platter

Preheat the oven to 375°.

Ask an adult to place the corn in the baking pan. Bake the corn for 20 minutes.

In a small bowl, stir together the chili powder and salt.

In another small bowl, whisk the mayonnaise with the lime juice.

5

Have an adult remove the corn from the oven. When cool enough to handle, brush the corn with the mayonnaise mixture.

6

Sprinkle the corn with the Parmesan cheese.

7 Sprinkle the corn with the chili powder mixture and serve.

MEAT & BEANS, MILK,
VEGETABLES, GRAINS

In Mexico, empanadas are often filled with meat and cheese, but Mexicans also make sweet versions for dessert.

Giant Taco Empanadas

INGREDIENTS
1 refrigerated pie crust
1 cup cooked taco meat
1/2 cup salsa
1/2 cup shredded
   cheddar cheese
1 large egg
1 tablespoon water

TOOLS
rimmed baking sheet
parchment paper
cooking spray
measuring cups
spoon
small bowl
measuring spoons
whisk
pastry brush
fork
oven mitts
pizza cutter
serving plates

Preheat the oven to 375°.

Line a rimmed baking sheet with parchment paper. Spray the paper with cooking spray.

Place the pie crust on the parchment paper.

Spread the taco meat on half of the pie crust, leaving a 1-inch border around the edge.

FUN WITH FOOD★ Add your favorite cooked vegetables to make your empanada extra healthy.

5

Spoon the salsa over the meat. Sprinkle the cheese over the salsa.

6

In a small bowl, whisk the egg with the water. Brush some of the egg mixture onto the bare half of the pie crust.

7

Fold the egg-brushed half of the pie crust over the other half. Press the edges together.

8

With a fork, press down around the edge of the pie crust to seal it.

9

Brush the empanada with the remaining egg mixture.

 10 Ask an adult to bake the empanada for 10 minutes, until golden brown. Use a pizza cutter to cut the empanada into wedges, and serve.

MEAT & BEANS, MILK, GRAINS, VEGETABLES

Burrito means "little donkey" in Spanish.

Wrap-n-Roll Burritos

INGREDIENTS

one 16-ounce can
   refried beans
1/2 teaspoon salt
1/2 teaspoon ground cumin
1 teaspoon chili powder
1/4 teaspoon dried oregano
2 teaspoons water
2 cups cooked rice
1/4 cup low-fat sour cream
eight 9-inch flour tortillas
1 cup salsa
6 lettuce leaves, torn
   into pieces
1/2 cup shredded
   cheddar cheese

TOOLS

small microwave-safe bowl
measuring spoons
wooden spoon
measuring cups
serving plate
platter

Place the refried beans in a small microwave-safe bowl. Add the salt, cumin, chili powder, oregano, and water. Stir well.

Ask an adult to microwave the bean mixture for 1 to 2 minutes, or until warm.

Stir in the rice and sour cream.

Place the tortillas on a serving plate and microwave them for 20 seconds.

FUN WITH FOOD★ Burritos make a great take-along lunch. Pack the fillings in plastic containers and the tortillas in a sandwich bag. Make the burritos when you're ready to eat.

5

Spread 1/2 cup of the bean mixture along the middle of a tortilla. Top with 2 tablespoons of salsa.

6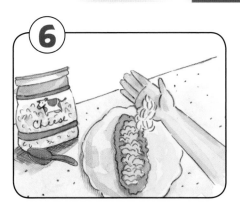

Sprinkle one-fourth of the lettuce and 2 tablespoons of the cheese on top of the beans.

7 Wrap the burrito closed. Repeat steps 5 and 6 to make the rest of the burritos, and serve.

This Recipe Includes

MEAT & BEANS, GRAINS, MILK, VEGETABLES

Originally, Mexican enchiladas were simply corn tortillas dipped in chili sauce.

Funky Chicken Enchiladas

INGREDIENTS

2 cooked chicken
  breasts, shredded
1/2 teaspoon ground cumin
1/2 teaspoon chili powder
1 teaspoon salt
1/2 cup chunky salsa
1 cup salsa verde
eight 6-inch corn tortillas
3/4 cup shredded
  cheddar cheese
low-fat sour cream,
  for serving

TOOLS

medium-sized mixing bowl
measuring spoons
measuring cups
2 wooden spoons
8-by-11-inch glass
  baking dish
oven mitts
platter

Preheat the oven to 350°.

Place the shredded chicken in a medium-sized mixing bowl. Add the cumin, chili powder, salt, and chunky salsa. Toss to combine.

Pour 1/2 cup of the salsa verde into the bottom of the baking dish.

Dip the tortillas in the salsa verde and set them aside (this helps to prevent them from cracking).

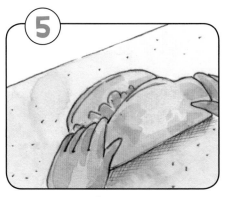

Place about 1/2 cup of shredded chicken along the middle of each tortilla and roll them closed.

Place the rolled tortillas in the baking dish, seam side down.

Pour the remaining salsa verde over the top of the tortillas.

Ask an adult to bake the enchiladas for 20 minutes and then remove them from the oven. Sprinkle the cheese over the enchiladas and bake for 10 minutes longer.

 Serve the enchiladas with the sour cream.

MEAT & BEANS, MILK, GRAINS, VEGETABLES

This Recipe Includes

In Mexico, tacos are traditionally made with soft tortillas.

Crispy Fish Tacos

INGREDIENTS
2 egg whites
1/2 cup coarse cornmeal
1 teaspoon salt
1/2 teaspoon freshly
   ground pepper
1 teaspoon chili powder
eight 4-ounce portions of
   fish, such as tilapia
   or trout
four 6-inch flour or corn
   tortillas, or 4 crispy
   taco shells
1/2 cup salsa
1 cup shredded taco cheese
2 cups shredded lettuce
8 lime wedges, for garnish

TOOLS
rimmed baking sheet
parchment paper
cooking spray
2 small mixing bowls
fork
measuring cups
measuring spoons
wooden spoon
oven mitts
metal spatula
platter

Preheat the oven to 400°.

Line a rimmed baking sheet with parchment paper and spray the paper with cooking spray.

In a small bowl, beat the egg whites with a fork until frothy.

Pour the cornmeal into another small bowl and stir in the salt, pepper, and chili powder.

24

NUTRITION NOTE★ Because the crispy fish in these tacos is baked, it's much healthier than fried fish.

5

Dip one fish fillet in the egg whites, then roll it in the cornmeal until coated. Place the fillet on the baking sheet, and repeat the process with the remaining fillets.

6

Ask an adult to bake the fish for 20 minutes or until cooked through and golden brown, turning the fillets over after 10 minutes.

7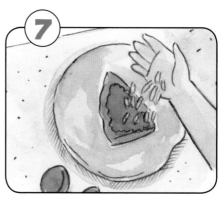

Place a fish fillet on each tortilla and top with 1 tablespoon of salsa and 2 tablespoons of cheese.

8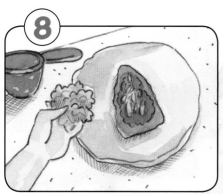

Top the cheese with 1/4 cup of lettuce.

9 Serve the tacos with the lime wedges.

VEGETABLES,
FRUITS, GRAINS

Guacamole was first made thousands of years ago by the Aztecs.

Guacamole-Filled Tomato Bowls

INGREDIENTS
4 large tomatoes
2 ripe avocados
2 tablespoons fresh
   lime juice
1/2 teaspoon cumin
1/2 teaspoon salt
1 tablespoon salsa
3 sprigs cilantro
tortilla chips, for serving

TOOLS
cutting board
serrated knife
melon baller
small, sharp knife
spoon
medium-sized mixing bowl
fork
measuring spoons
wooden spoon
kitchen shears
platter

Ask an adult to cut off the top 1/2 inch of each tomato with a serrated knife.

With a melon baller, scoop out the insides of the tomatoes.

With a small knife, cut an avocado in half lengthwise. (Note: Cut around the pit.)

Twist the two avocado halves to separate them. Repeat with the other avocado.

NUTRITION NOTE★ Avocados are full of heart-healthy fats and potassium.

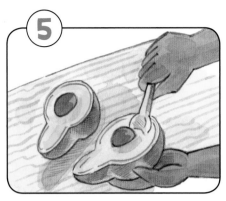

Scoop out the avocado pits. Then scoop out the avocado insides with a spoon. Place the insides in a medium-sized mixing bowl.

Mash the avocado insides with a fork.

Add the lime juice, cumin, salt, and salsa to the bowl. Stir until combined.

With a kitchen shears, snip the cilantro into small pieces and stir into the guacamole.

Spoon the guacamole into the tomato bowls.

Serve the guacamole with tortilla chips.

GRAINS,
MEAT & BEANS

This Recipe Includes

These light, crunchy cookies are called *biscochitos* in Mexico.

Wedding Cookies

INGREDIENTS

1 stick unsalted
   butter, softened
1/2 cup confectioners'
   sugar
1/4 cup cornstarch
1/4 teaspoon pure
   vanilla extract
3/4 cup all-purpose flour
1/3 cup chopped pecans
   or almonds

TOOLS

rimmed baking sheet
cooling rack
parchment paper
medium-sized mixing bowl
wooden spoon
measuring cups
measuring spoons
oven mitts
metal spatula
small bowl
platter

Preheat the oven to 350°.

Line a rimmed baking sheet and
cooling rack with parchment paper.

In a medium-sized mixing bowl,
stir the butter with 1/4 cup of the
confectioners' sugar until smooth.

Add the cornstarch, vanilla,
flour, and nuts. Stir until a soft
dough forms.

28

Form the dough into about 12 balls. Transfer the balls to the baking sheet.

Ask an adult to bake the cookies on the center rack of the oven for about 20 minutes, until the bottoms are golden brown. With a spatula, transfer the cookies to the rack.

Pour the remaining confectioners' sugar into a small bowl.

While the cookies are still warm, roll them in the confectioners' sugar. Place them back on the rack to cool.

9 Let the cookies cool completely, then serve.

MILK, FRUITS, MEAT & BEANS

This moist, creamy dessert is named for the three kinds of milk used to soak the cake.

Tres Leches Cake

INGREDIENTS
one 18-ounce box yellow
   cake mix
3 large eggs
1 1/4 cup water
1/3 cup vegetable oil
1 teaspoon vanilla extract
one 14-ounce can sweetened
   condensed milk
one 12-ounce can low-fat
   evaporated milk
1 cup low-fat milk
2 cups whipped cream
2 cups sliced strawberries

TOOLS
9-by-13-inch baking pan
cooking spray
large mixing bowl
whisk
clear measuring cup
measuring spoons
oven mitts
medium-sized mixing bowl
wooden skewer
plastic wrap
rubber spatula
small, sharp knife
serving plates

30

Preheat the oven to 350°.

Spray a 9-by-13-inch baking pan with cooking spray.

In a large bowl, whisk the cake mix with the eggs, water, oil, and vanilla until smooth.

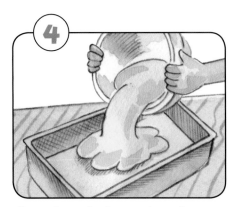

Pour the cake batter into the pan.

FOOD FACT★ In Italy, there's a similar dessert called tiramisu that is soaked in coffee.

5 Ask an adult to bake the cake for 35 minutes or until golden brown. Remove the cake from the oven and let cool for 10 minutes.

6 In a medium-sized mixing bowl, whisk together the sweetened condensed milk, evaporated milk, and low-fat milk until blended.

7 Using a wooden skewer, poke holes in the cake. Pour the milk mixture over the cake.

8 Cover the cake in plastic wrap, and refrigerate it for at least 1 hour.

9 With a rubber spatula, spread the whipped cream over the cake. Top the cake with the sliced strawberries.

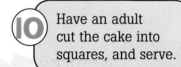

10 Have an adult cut the cake into squares, and serve.

INDEX

ON THE WEB

FactHound offers a safe, fun way to find educator-approved
Internet sites related to this book.

Here's what you do:
    1. Visit *www.facthound.com*
    2. Choose your grade level.
    3. Begin your search.

This book's ID number is 9781404851894

KIDS DISH